On This Mountain

On This Mountain

Essays on Ten Welsh Mountains

images by
Ray Wood

Published in 2008 by
Gomer Press, Llandysul, Ceredigion SA44 4JL
www.gomer.co.uk

ISBN 9781843239161

A CIP record for this title is available from the British Library

This book is published with the financial support of the
Welsh Books Council.

Printed and bound in Wales at
Gomer Press, Llandysul, Ceredigion

'…ye shall serve God upon this mountain.'
Exodus 3$^{12}$

'And he will destroy in this mountain the face of the
covering cast over all people…'
Isaiah 25$^{7}$

'Our fathers worshipped in this mountain.'
John 4$^{20}$

# CONTENTS

# PREFACE

## Bethan Mair

What is a mountain? Leafing through this book, it is possible to contest that some of the ten mountains so lovingly portrayed here hardly constitute hills, let alone mountains. If size alone matters, then the argument is already lost; but sometimes a mountain becomes a mountain for reasons other than its sheer mass. Stark statistics, which can call a Munro a Munro in Scotland or, come to that, a Marilyn in England and Wales, cut no ice with the authors of this collection. To them, each of the ten are mountains, as much in the spiritual and metaphysical sense as in any strictly geographical sense.

When faced with the task of inviting just ten Welsh authors to write about their favourite mountain, we were faced with – pardon the pun – an uphill struggle. In a politically-correct way, we aimed for gender balance and a parity between north and south Wales. Some names were unavoidable – especially Dr Angharad Price, whose masterpiece of Welsh prose, *O! Tyn y Gorchudd*, was the inspiration for the initial idea that grew into this book. A forebear of hers, Hugh Jones, Maesglasau (1749–1825) wrote the hymn that begins with the words

> *O! tyn*
> *Y gorchudd yn y mynydd hyn:*
> (Pull back
> The veil from on this mountain)

– a powerful image borrowed from the Old Testament's Book of Isaiah. It would be impossible to imagine this collection without a contribution by Angharad, so she was the first name on the list, but the other nine swiftly followed. The accomplished authors were given the freedom to choose their favourite mountain and, serendipitously, their selection gave an opportunity to go to the four corners of Wales. The next, crucial step would be to illustrate the words.

Ray Wood is a world-class mountaineering and outdoor photographer. He and his family live in Dinorwig, in the heart of Snowdonia, where he can easily indulge his passion for climbing. We felt he was the natural choice for this volume so we were extremely fortunate to secure a grant from the Welsh Books Council to commission Ray to make these images, which were all created specifically for this book.

If the photographer is well known as a climber, the authors are not all seasoned mountaineers: they were selected for their aptitude as wordsmiths rather than for their knowledge of the crampon and the carabiner. Nevertheless, each has chosen to share their experiences of being out on the mountains they portray, so that we, whether we be mountaineers, walkers or even leisurely armchair enthusiasts, can share the magic of these distant, lonely, uplifting places.

On This Mountain

# MYNYDD TYNYBRAICH
## Angharad Price

Tynybraich: the name belongs to a house and a mountain; to a family too, at least in local speech. They have been farming Tynybraich for centuries, my mother's forefathers. There's a genealogy in the family Bible, branches of men's names dating back to 1012.

We came to Tynybraich every school holiday, leaving the quarries of Arfon behind us and heading south. To Dinas Mawddwy, where we learned how to live with mountains, not against them. Turning off the main road, we saw flowers reaching for the car and rabbits running from it. Coming out from Y Ffridd we looked down at the Maesglasau valley and across to Tynybraich mountain, a pyramid of blue extending upwards from the narrow valley floor. In the distance, the rock of Maesglasau, its waterfall our vertical horizon.

We didn't care for the mountain, which we took for granted. We cared only for the house. After all, it was the house that gave the mountain its name. Tynybraich: 'House in the Mountain's Arm.' It was our grandparents' home and we were keen to get there. But there was the steep hill to descend, the brook to cross, the other hill to ascend, seeing nothing ahead but the car bonnet and some sky. Dogs would rush and bark at the sound of unfamiliar wheels.

Only Nan could calm us again. Our mother's mother, waiting for us at the farmhouse door, touched by the smell of food that came through the kitchen window.

She'd come to Dinas Mawddwy in wartime to visit a cousin. My grandfather, Taid, was newly widowed, nearly forty and a father of two. Nan never returned to her home in Cwm Nant yr Eira, the Valley of Snow, in neighbouring Montgomeryshre. On the day they were married she became a wife, a farm wife, a stepmother and a daughter-in-law all at once. Nan began her life at Tynybraich, soon herself to become a mother of two.

Taid insisted she learn to drive. She was to be self-sufficient. At her first outing, with fresh snow on the ground, the car veered off the mountain road and skidded to the edge of the ravine. He straightened the car and forced his young wife to drive back to the house. It was much later that she thanked him for his lesson. For the rest of her life, the car was her means of escape from Tynybraich. Every Wednesday she went to Machynlleth in it, and every Friday to Dolgellau; and to her sister's in Arthog on Saturday night. The car took her to the village on social visits, or in condolence. She delivered meals-on-wheels to old age pensioners.

She was at her most independent in the car. At election time, she'd draw out her Plaid Cymru poster from the glove compartment. When Tynybraich was out of sight, she'd stick it on the windscreen and drive around – a raging nationalist. Returning to Tynybraich, just before Y Ffridd, the poster was folded up and put away. Taid was Labour. There would have been trouble, for there was nothing he liked more than a good debate, and nothing she liked less.

She was an even-tempered woman. The evenness spread out from her. She organised her world evenly around her. Her kitchen table was an even cosmos: planets of plates and saucers, lids of jam jars, Welsh cakes, a Victoria sponge and rounds of bread and butter. Spoons and knives shone like stars between them.

She baked her Welsh cakes every morning, rolling out the speckled dough over the table, a continent whose boundaries stretched outwards from the middle, barely visibly, as the rolling pin moved lightly under Nan's hand. Our anxiety as the rounds were cut out. Pained again as the golden dough was stained on the griddle. Nan just smiled and carried on. She must have made thousands of them in her life, those golden coins, but statistics would be meaningless. Nan wasn't one to keep count.

The evenness of her handiwork. The swift movement of knitting needles, the controlled loosening and tightening of the wool under her finger. She threw off the stitches carelessly, discarding them as she talked and laughed. But at cast-off and make-up, the stitches' uniform tension proved her even hand.

Remnants of clothing were transformed into patchwork quilts. We watched her do it. Her endless patience. Tracing the aluminium template. Cutting up the hexagons. Tacking. Stitching hexagon to hexagon. Time becoming space. Daily life made even.

Nan created a garden for herself at the back of the farmhouse, a patch of mountain enclosed by a wire fence. The Italian prisoners of war helped her, showing how to carve terraces into the earth, as they'd done in their own vineyards. Nan grew flowers and shrubs, in counterpoint to the mountain, like the Latin plants' names and her accent.

But the earth was rough and shingly, unfavourable to horticulture. The mountain tended to reclaim its own ground. The terraces became steeper. But Nan persisted. The garden was her pride.

Sheep would push through, eating all that was edible, trampling on the terraces, leaving behind them nothing but grassless patches. Of course, she'd been foolish to challenge the mountain. But soon the flowers were back. Nan too held her ground.

Mynydd Tynybraich

On This Mountain

She was even in walk and even in talk, and even also in grace. Who could have told that she'd spent her life between two mountains?

Nan watched us playing from the farmhouse window. The mountain had lessons to teach, especially to those of us who'd been reared on marshland. It pulled itself from beneath us, made us somersault through thistles, wool and sheep shit.

Back in the house we found our feet again. The quiet of the hearth. We stared into the fire. Butter melted in a glass dish. Nan would be laying the table.

Then Taid came in cold from the mountain, the stub of a *Players* cigarette between finger and thumb. He wheezed as he approached. Our chatter stopped. Between snatches of breath we'd hear him talk of the mountain.

At the top there were bilberry bushes and pools of water where people had dug for peat. There were larks rising and peregrines falling. The steep Oerddrws Pass, far below, seemed flat. And above there were nothing but peaks: Waun Oer, Foel y Ffridd, Foel Bendin, y Glasgwm, Aran Fawddwy, Aran Benllyn, Cader Idris . . . Taid knew all their names.

He'd talk about superstitions. The words were unfamiliar: 'cotton grass', 'the bandits', 'causeway' . . . There was that sprig of white heather, and the strange flower that swallowed flies. We couldn't disbelieve him. And yet, we couldn't quite believe him either. Taid's testament was ambiguous, he himself so foreign to us.

After supper he fetched his broken glasses and retired to the parlour to read. He adored debates: books on history and politics. His horizons were broad; you'd think he'd always lived on a mountain top. We'd look at him as we looked towards the summit of Tynybraich, obliquely and from a distance. And as with the mountain, we sought his attention and feared it. The steep banks of his personality: his strict attitudes and his laughter at men's folly.

Of course we didn't know of Taid the shepherd. His daily care for the sheep on the mountain, climbing through the seasons to perpetuate the work of his forefathers.

Between winter and spring, billhook in hand, he'd cut off branches to feed the sheep. At lambing he'd be up there counting, protecting the weak from crows and foxes. A late frost, threatening sleet, Taid would come home with a lamb in his pocket, all damp and slippery, its breath irregular and its head hanging down. It was placed on the hearth in a box lined with newspaper, nourished by Taid with milk from a rubber teat. Nain watched from a distance, new life dirtying the hearthstone.

In spring, if the kitchen light diminished, Taid climbed up to the reservoir at the top of the mountain. It was frogspawn stopping the flow of water down to the turbine. He'd move it away by the fistful, keeping one for the jar which he'd bring back to his children, a transparent treasure. And the kitchen was lit up anew.

Weaning time, and Taid would have to separate the male lambs from their mothers. For days the mothers would bleat, Taid watching them press their bodies against the bars of the mountain gate.

With his neighbours he'd gather sheep for dipping and shearing, relaxing at the end of the day with banter at the kitchen table, Nan half-listening as she refilled the dinner plates.

But it was in winter that the mountain demanded most from Taid. Sheep would be trapped under the snow. He climbed up, inserting a rod made of hazel through the thick snow. Prodding and poking, he knew from experience where the sheep sheltered. But there was no guarantee. Finally, feeling the living softness, he'd go down on all fours to release it. Then he'd watch it escape, chunks of snow hanging off the wool, shining in the blue light.

Hours later Taid would return home, lame with frostbite. Nan, relieved, would fetch her husband a bowl of hot stock.

We didn't know how much the mountain had demanded from Taid. My mother's brother had taken over by the time we came along. We were too young to have heard the story of Taid's three brothers, born blind, sent away to a boarding school far away in Worcester, and of two other brothers, dead, as well as a sister dead, his only sister. Taid had been the only one left to work on the farm, to continue as his forefathers had. At eleven years of age Tynybraich had demanded his life.

Gravity's strict lessons, Taid learnt them when he was eleven. Tynybraich tried to possess his life, his education and his wish to study medicine. But he reached a compromise with the mountain, dividing his life between it and his fellow men. He became a councillor, a Union man, and travelled on business to London and Brussels.

An unwilling farmer, he nevertheless wrote his name in the family Bible, and in local speech, at least, took on the mountain's name. After their marriage, Nan shared that name with him. Tynybraich: covenant of mountain and house.

I only climbed it once, Tynybraich. Taid had been buried many years, Nan a few months. His testament was there at the top: the bilberry bushes, the water pools, the lark and the

Mynydd Tynybraich

peregrine, the Pass, the bandits, the cotton grass, the causeway, and those peaks whose names I didn't know.

A feeling of trespassing made me leave. In any case I had to go, saying goodbye to my aunt and uncle and turning my back on Tynybraich, driving back to the main road, heading south, towards Cardiff. Tomorrow was work.

I picked my way through thistles, wool and sheep shit. As I came within sight of the house, I slowed down, as Taid himself would have done, and let myself be drawn by the farmhouse's gravity. There was the sound of Nan laying the table.

I wondered at the narrow ledge on which the house stood. The precipice beneath. And I saw, as Taid himself would have seen, the evenness spreading out from the house and filling the valley.

Mynydd Tynybraich

On This Mountain

# MYNYDD Y GWRHYD
## Alun Wyn Bevan

It's strange how a previously innocuous date can suddenly take on a huge significance in one's life, be it a wedding day, a child's birthday, or even a great sporting occasion. In my case the date in question was Friday, July 7, 1978.

As headteacher at Ystradowen County Primary School in Cwmllynfell, it was my usual practice on a Friday afternoon to take charge of the ten and eleven-year-olds – those young pupils who would soon leave the cloistered environment of the small village school to embark on a new experience at the vastly bigger Amman Valley Comprehensive School at Ammanford. While we were discussing various issues (not necessarily those specified in the current National Curriculum, I might add) a fresh-faced young girl, Mari Nest Williams, raised her arm.

'Are you going on the walk tomorrow, sir?'

'And what walk would that be?'

'A new organisation has been formed in the area and they're all interested in birds and flowers and the general environment. They're going on their very first walk and I thought you might be going.'

Further enquiries revealed that the walk would start at the road bridge at Brynhenllys and follow a route which would hopefully end at the source of the River Twrch. With more than a hint of embarrassment, I had to confess that I would not be attending as I had been selected to play cricket for Ammanford. Although the class accepted my explanation, I felt somewhat unsettled – here was an eleven-year-old, keen to learn more about the surrounding area while her headteacher put more store on a sporting commitment!

I slept fitfully that night, torn between my desire to indulge my sporting passion and the need to do the right thing by the pupils. I need not have worried because, as Saturday dawned, the decision was made for me. During the night the heavens had opened and a leaden sky meant that no cricket would be played on this particular Saturday.

And so at ten thirty, armed with a flask of coffee, some ham rolls and an apple, I set off ready to join the walkers. I soon came to realise that these individuals were as passionate about their subject as I was about sport – and, what is more, this enthusiasm was infectious. Their knowledge of the flora and fauna was truly incredible and I hung on their every word. In fact, by the end of the morning I was well and truly hooked!

To my shame, I could not believe that there was so much to see and so much to learn and all within an Ian Botham drive from the school where I had worked for the last few years. I think this is true of many of us – proud to say we have broadened our horizons by visiting far-away places and yet totally ignorant of the wonders to marvel at on our own doorstep.

Thankfully, I had remembered to take a notebok to record details of the expedition (mainly so that I could recount them to the children the following week) and this has now become one of my most treasured possessions. We saw birch and willow trees, small cudweed, hawk bit, bird's foot trefoil, wood ragwort, wild thyme, red and white clover, mare's tail, cow wheat, and helleborine. Turning those pages is akin to replaying a reel of film, and the memories of that magical day come flooding back.

Ystradowen was a typical mining village in South Wales, littered with the detritus of the coal industry but surrounded by the beauty of the Black Mountains and the Gwrhyd mountain. It's true that I had often gazed out of the classroom windows and admired the beauty of these mountains but had never taken the time to explore them in great depth.

Now amongst the slurry of the abandoned coal tips, I was shown some hidden gems, defiantly growing against all the odds. As the party made its way towards the river, we came across two types of oak trees, *quercus petrea* and *quercus robur*. Here also the green oak moth was enjoying a hearty meal at the expense of the oak leaves.

Crossing over to the Carmarthenshire side of the river, we came across a lone aspen tree, *populus tremola* and those experts in our midst were astonished to find in the gorge at

Pwll y Berw examples of royal fern, male fern, green spleenwort and the majestic globe flower. As we walked on in the general direction of Llwyncwmstabl, we passed several derelict farms, many now reduced to piles of rubble while others were almost completely hidden by the undergrowth. In their heyday these had been successful concerns going by the names of Pen-y-wern, Gellïau, Derlwyn Isaf, and Sarn-fân.

Despite the driving rain and the wind gusting in our faces, it was a determined group that eventually made its way to the source of the River Twrch. On the final stage of the walk, we had negotiated our steps between the many streams that spewed out from Pen-yr-Helyg, the crystal clear waters hurtling haphazardly towards the river below. It had been a truly unforgettable day, and I could not wait to get home and share my experiences with the rest of the family.

Over the next few weeks I spent a small fortune buying books on wildlife, plants, ordnance-survey maps and the like. This was in the fervent hope that I could learn as much as possible about the environment, and not look like a complete ignoramus in the company of such well-informed naturalists.

My friends and family were astonished to find that henceforth sport was not the most important activity on Saturdays – rather I became a faithful member of *Cymdeithas Edward Llwyd*, and with my two children in tow we spent some of the most enjoyable times of my life exploring the countryside. It is thanks to Mari Nest and such esteemed personae as Dafydd Dafis, Twm Elias, Duncan Brown, Ann Thomas, Rosanne Alexander and the late Ted Breeze Jones, Wil Jones and Dillwyn Roberts that a whole new world opened up to me. I have been fortunate through my work to

travel the globe: I have admired the mighty Andes, the scenic Rockies, the secrets of Kerala, the Norwegian glaciers, the beauty of Lesotho, the wonders of Petra and Jaresh in the Middle East, but there is still one place I return to again and again, a mere stone's throw from the Black Mountains – the Gwrhyd Mountain.

I would hazard a guess that not many people in Wales know of its existence – it fact it hardly appears on an O.S. map. For anyone, therefore, who may be interested in visiting this beautiful area, I should explain that it occupies the territory between the villages of Cwmllynfell and Rhyd-y-Fro on the western fringe of West Glamorgan. Using Brynaman as a starting point and travelling east, the first village one passes through is Cefn Bryn Brain – the birthplace of Professor Derec Llwyd Morgan and Mair Lewis (the mother of Josh Lewsey, the England rugby international and World Cup winner). The next village is Cwmllynfell, which boasts poets Ben Davies and Watcyn Wyn as two famous sons. Halfway through the village and bisecting the chapel and the school, a right-hand turn leads to the Gwrhyd mountain. As the road begins its ascent, to the right stands the old Mountain Hare Inn (known locally as 'Y Boblen') which for years served as the village rugby club thanks to its proximity to the playing field. This has to be one of the most exposed and rugged playing surfaces in the Northern Hemisphere.

Incidentally, it was at Cwmllynfell that the pioneering sports broadcaster Eic Davies spent many a Saturday afternoon, pen and notebook in hand, recording the highlights of the afternoon's play before making a mad dash in his faithful Rover 75 to the BBC studios in Swansea to give his customary Saturday evening report. Eic, of course, was a son of the Gwrhyd having been born in a smallholding, 'Y Parc'.

Other sons of the Gwrhyd would have trod a diffrent path and ended their careers as miners in the many small collieries that dotted the hillside. Others would cross the common to search for work at the Steer, East Pit and Maerdy collieries at Tairgwaith near Gwauncaegurwen. It was a time of great hardship when many young lives were lost in the dark bowels of the mines. The anthracite coal extracted here was considered to be of the highest quality and it is said that there were stoves in the USA and Canada engraved with the words 'Use GCG coal only'.

Leaving the rugby ground and the scars of the industrial valley behind, the road leads onto the mountain and for a short distance all one can see is hundreds of sheep dotted around like white spots on the horizon, and the ruins of what were once small homesteads. These give way once more to the skeletal remains of three more small mines – the Gover, the Glen and Gwaith y Tyle. It is said that one of the owners of the Gover Colliery led something of a dual life – he was an educated gentleman, a Geology professor in the Middle East, but when the need arose, he would exchange his academic cap for a helmet, handing out practical advice and support at the Welsh coal face.

Until the 1980s, as one followed the winding road towards Coedffaldau, it was possible to glimpse the coal tip at Cwmllynfell. Thanks to the government's regeneration programme, this has now been cleared and the area landscaped. Astonishingly some sections of the community disapproved of this scheme at the time – citing the fact that the coal tips served as a reminder to future generations of the hardships endured by their ancestors.

At the bottom of Tyle'r Roc (birthplace of the poet Dyfnallt Owen), a narrow lane leads towards the sleepy hamlet of Rhiwfawr. Within a short distance of this fork in the road and near the boundary with Hendreforgan Farm, one happens upon a panorama which takes one's breath away. This is seen at its best during the autumn when the kaleidoscopic colours rival any seen in New England in the fall. As the eye follows the horizon, it is possible to see in the distance the demerara-coloured hills surrounding Llyn-y-Fan and the source of the rivers Tawe, Usk, Haffes, Giedd, Gwys and Twrch.

Among many that have been hypnotised by this vista is the actor Peter O'Toole, whose ex-wife Sian Phillips was a native of the area. The locals would have it that the star of the film *Lawrence of Arabia* enjoyed nothing more than to spend a leisurely summer evening, a pint of Evans Bevan in hand, relaxing in the company of miners and friends. Sadly the doors of the Rock Tavern closed for the last time in the 1960s and the building is now slowly decaying as the ravages of time take their toll.

One last steep incline up the notorious Cilfer Hill and we reach the top of the mountain. The gradient here is such that it provides a challenge for even the most powerful of 4x4s. One can only imagine how the Morris Minors and Jowett Javelins of yesteryear fared against such odds. Nevertheless, having overcome this last hurdle, the rewards are well worth the effort. The views are breathtaking and on a clear day it's possible to see the Brecon Beacons which includes y Fan Hir, Fan Gyhirych, Fan Nedd, Pen-y-Fan, and Craig-y-Llyn above Glyn-neath.

After this glorious panorama, the journey continues in the direction of Rhyd-y-Fro. The rocky landscape stretches for mile upon mile and an eerie silence seems to hang like a veil over the place giving the impression that this is virgin territory, undiscovered by man. Yet, here and there, a few bleak reminders of man's interference with nature jolts one back to reality. The small mines of Bryngorof, Park Level, and Tir Bach

Mynydd y Gwrhyd

On This Mountain

lay abandoned alongside the barren waste created by futile attempts at extracting coal by opencast mining. Nearby is Troedrhiwfelen Farm, just a field's breadth from a cottage called Cae Du Uchaf. Until it burnt to the ground in the 1950s, this was the home of Rhys Haydn Williams's grandparents. R. H. Williams played in the second row for Llanelli, Wales and the British Lions, and while touring New Zealand in 1959, he was described by the legendary Colin Meads as the best player of his generation.

A few hundred yards further along, a small track leads off in the direction of Gelliwarog Farm and an accompanying small mine run by the two brothers who lived there. The location of the smallholding was so remote as to cause some embarrassment for a visiting Inspector of Mines who spent a whole morning trying to find the place. When he eventually happened upon it, he was confronted with a tricky situation. It was his duty to ensure the care and safety of the miners and that all procedures were in place and strictly adhered to:

'Where's your safety equipment? Where's your stretcher?' were the questions asked. Will, the older brother disappeared momentarily, returning with a wheelbarrow.

'This is the only stretcher needed here sir. There are only two of us!'

What the Inspector of Mines made of it all was not recorded in the official report.

Returning to the main road brings Gwrhyd Chapel into view – a plain, simple building which has provided a spiritual and physical haven for the inhabitants of the Gwrhyd mountain over the centuries. When biting winds sweep across the landscape, many a traveller has taken refuge within its sturdy walls. Across the road from the chapel lie the ruins of what was once a school and, latterly, an isolation hospital for infectious diseases.

In the distance it is possible to pick out several farmhouses – Cwmnantstafell, Cwmnantllici, Gellifowy, Crachlwyn, Pentwyn, Perthigwynion, Llwynpryfed, Fforchegel (where my grandmother was born and which is also home to the family of the naturalist Iolo Williams), Gwrhyd Uchaf, Gellilwca, y Pant and Ynys-wen. On the brow of the hill stands Blaenegel Farm and below the river Egel splutters its way down the valley to join the Clydach at Rhyd-y-Fro and the Tawe at Pontardawe. As the road begins its descent, one is made aware that civilization is never far away. The grey, barren waste around Pontardawe has long disappeared and has been replaced by the new factories and business parks of the twenty-first century.

Perhaps it is a travesty that the Gwrhyd has not been included on many atlases, but there are those of us who are grateful for the omission.

On This Mountain

# CADER IDRIS
## Bethan Gwanas

I've been around the world three times now (honestly, I've followed the equator the whole way around, as well as the latitude 52° line, and been to the South Pole and back up the other side via the North Pole); I've seen the Rockies, the Andes, the Alps, the Urals, the Cairngorms, the Picos, the Pyrenees, the Ellsworth Mountain range and many other mountains whose names escape me, but not one of them is half as special to me as Cader Idris. Snowdon may be higher and more famous, but in my opinion, she's the ugly sister to Cader's Cinderella.

In the 1695 version of *Britannica Camden*, it was claimed that Cader Idris, and not Ben Nevis, was the highest mountain in Britain, and people believed this for years. In the 1720s, Daniel Defoe wrote that he had seen 'the famous Cader-Idricks which some are of the opinion is the highest mountain in Britain'. Unfortunately, they found that this wasn't so – by a long way – but size isn't everything, and I'll say it again: no other peak can touch Cader Idris. Alright, maybe the fact that I was born and brought up at the foot of Cader may have something to do with that view, but people from miles away have agreed with me. 'I lay there in silence; a spirit came over

me . . .' said the poet Mrs Hemans in the mid 1800s, '. . . things glorious, unearthly, passed floating before me.' Peacock, who wrote in the same era, believed that this was 'The land of all that is beautiful in nature'. Yes, there's definitely something about Cader Idris.

There's the name for starters. Cader Idris means Idris's Chair. But who was Idris? Some say he was a giant, but according to others, he was one of three astronomers who were so clever they could could foretell the future. The other two were Gwydion ap Dôn and Gwyn ap Nudd, but the summit was named after Idris. They say that he used to sit there, studying the stars, and that the rock was eventually worn down to the shape of his backside. Yet another school of thought suggests that it was the old way of calling educated men 'giants' that gave birth to the legend. But many firmly believed that he was a real giant and that '*y tri graienyn*' – the three pebbles – were proof enough. These were three very large rocks that used to be at the top of Bwlch Tal-y-llyn, which were apparently thrown there when Idris stopped in pain whilst walking one day, took off his shoe and found the three pebbles inside. There used to be a small lake at this spot too, Llyn y Tri

Graienyn, but when they built the new road over the pass, the lake was filled in and two of the rocks were blasted away. The original name for the pass was Bwlch y Llyn Bach ('pass of the small lake') but as the lake sadly no longer exists, it's now called Bwlch Tal-y-llyn.

There used to be quite a few fairy folk on and around Cader Idris, some more pleasant than others. A particularly nasty one was the Little Green Man of Gwernan Lake. He used to smile to himself as he watched people climbing towards the summit, then he would conjure up mists and storms and shout *'Daeth yr awr!'*, 'The hour has come!' The unfortunate climbers would fall over the cliffs to their deaths, and the Little Green Man would collect their battered bodies and drag them down to the deepest, darkest depths of Llyn Gwernan. Strangely enough, the lake bubbles rather disturbingly during really hot summers. I'll let your imagination decide whether it's the algae or the Little Green Man . . .

During the eighteenth and nineteenth centuries, it became fashionable for the well-off (Kilvert and Tennyson among them) to come to this area to holiday in the wild and romantic setting. But Kilvert wasn't that impressed: 'The stoniest, dreariest, most desolate mountain I was ever on,' said the miserable old sod.

But everyone else loved it here. By 1784, a local guide by the name of Robin Edwards had been taking people up Cader for forty years.

The Victorian visitors were delighted when a small hut was built on the summit in the 1830s. By 1869, anything between 40 and 60 ponies were available in stables in Dolgellau to carry lazy people up the mountain, and several local men used to offer their services as guides. One especially colourful character had prepared his own leaflet. I'm not sure whether he had swallowed a dictionary or whether he had asked a rather mischievous visitor to write it on his behalf, but this is what was written on the leaflet:

> Guide general and magnificent expounder of all the natural and artificial curiosities of North Wales, professor of grand and bombastical lexicographical words; knight of the most anomalous, whimsical, yet perhaps, happy order of hair-brained inexplicables.

Many people are confused as to which of the four summits is Cader itself. So here's the answer: from the east and the direction of Tal-y-llyn, the first summit is Geugraig or Gau Graig (also called Mynydd Werngraig), then Mynydd Moel, and next is Pen y Gader – the highest summit – then you have

Cader Idris

On This Mountain

Cyfrwy and y Tyrau Mawr stretching out towards the sea. They form a semicircle which is described perfectly in this verse by Wil Ifan:

> . . . *A'r hen fynyddoedd, gawr a chawr,*
> *O'u cylch yn gwmni wedi cwrdd,*
> *A'u peneliniau ar y bwrdd*
> *Uwchben eu hoesol broblem fawr.*

The last two lines descibe the mountains as giants with their elbows on the table, pondering life's eternal problems.

The best route? Well, some paths are easier than others, but none are easy. My favourite is Minffordd: it's steep but gorgeous and takes you past Llyn Cau – one of the most glorious views on earth, painted by great artists over the years, including Richard Wilson in 1765. I have a wonderful print by Wiliam Selwyn on my kitchen wall, and several of my friends have fallen in love with it and bought their own copies. This is where my grandfather, Llewelyn Evans, would come with his neighbours to bring the sheep down from the mountain. The most popular route is the Pony track, but the original Welsh name was Llwybr Pilin Pwn, according to the late Tommy Price who was brought up in Pen-y-bryn, Cwm Hafod Oer. And the Welsh name for Foxes Path is Llwybr Madyn, a route which is not for the fainthearted. It's very steep and all scree. These old Welsh names are seldom used, so please start using them. It would be a crime if they disappeared for ever.

I was a schoolgirl when I first went up Cader. It was a school trip, in the days when we were encouraged to appreciate what was on our doorstep, not sent in busloads all the way to Alton Towers. It was a sweltering day of summer, not a cloud in the sky and it was magical. I swam in Llyn y Gader on the way back and it was breathtakingly cold; I remember that climbing back out made me feel as if I'd been scrubbed all over with a toothbrush.

I've been up many times after that, sometimes with groups of friends, sometimes on my own; sometimes in the rain, sometimes in sunshine; but the best times by far were in the snow. You have to time things well in winter as the days are so much shorter and climbing back down in the dark is not a good idea. You have to prepare yourself properly too, and wear the appropriate gear. I remember one of my friends once met me in Minffordd in a pair of moccasins – in winter!

Whenever I set off in winter, the summit is hidden by thick cloud. But Cader has always been kind to me and often by the time I've reached the top, the wind has blown away the clouds, leaving blue skies and glorious views of Meirionnydd under a sparkling carpet of snow. On other days, this mountain lets me climb for miles through icy mists, freezing my hair into icicles and frosting my eyelashes, before allowing me to step up to the summit and rise above the clouds. And then I just can't stop myself from smiling like an idiot: it's wonderful, a sea of clouds below me, stretching for ever towards the horizon and the other peaks of Snowdonia gleaming like shark fins in the distance. At times like these, who would want to live anywhere else?

It's worth looking around at the views that surround you: to the east is Bwlch yr Oerddrws, where the leaders of Wales met to discuss what to do next on the death of Owain Glyn Dŵr. It's said that a kind of peasant court was held here regularly, and that there used to be gallows here. Further to the east, is Llanymawddwy, where Baron Owen was killed on October 11, 1555, by Gwylliaid Cochion Mawddwy, the red-haired bandits who used to rob and terrorize travellers. There's a cave up there somewhere, called Ogof y Lladron, Cave of Thieves, where they used to hide before attacking. It's very well hidden, too, because I've never found it.

The route taken by the stagecoach from London came through Bwlch yr Oerddrws, but as it's so steep and such hard work for the horses, the travellers would have to dismount at the bottom of the pass and walk all the way to the top, complaining with every step. I can't blame them. But I'm sure they appreciated the view once they got there.

Closer to us is Tir Ystent, where a man called Coch y Fedw was born, the strongest man in Wales in his time. When six of the strongest men in the area failed to lift a large beam above a new fireplace, Coch managed to place it there perfectly all on his own; but then, they do say his mother breastfed him until he was fifteen years old!

To the north is Dolgellau: 'Within the town, not a single road deserves to be thus called,' said Idris Fychan in 1872. He went on to say that should one climb up one of the many hills around the town, one would see 'merely a collection of dwellings, looking as if they had fallen willy nilly from the summit of Cader Idris.' Today, over two hundred buildings in Dolgellau are listed as being of historical or architectural interest; more than any other town in Wales.

'Until the mid-eighteenth century, the morals and activities within the town were very low,' said Idris Fychan in 1872. There were nine fairs every year, '. . . which involved fist fights, cockerel fights and running (men and women). The fights were of a very brutal nature, especially between the men of Llanfachreth and Dolgellau. These were not fights between two men but mobs with sticks and stones, and the wounds were so terrible, many met their deaths after fighting in Dolgellau. We were also told that the clergy and Justices of the Peace were often ringleaders, urging men to join in the battle. Most towns behaved thus in those days, but Dolgellau was renowned for being one of the worst.'

Cader Idris

The cockerel fights used to take place where the cricket pitch lies today; it was also the spot where the men of Dolgellau and Llanfachreth beat each other to a pulp for many years. The feud started because of an argument between two prominent families: the Owen family of Y Llwyn (an old people's home today) and that of Huw Nannau Hen. They all ended up in court when one of the servants of Nannau was killed in June 1601 whilst playing bowls on the Marian – a green in the centre of the town used for less perilous pursuits these days. The Llwyn family was found guilty but nobody was actually punished. Both sides carried on destroying each other's property, stealing cattle and smashing in heads for many years. You will be relieved to hear that they all get on very well these days.

Nannau is further north in Llanfachreth, and is the highest mansion in Wales, apparently. The original building was burnt to the ground by Owain Glyn Dŵr who was understandably upset when his cousin, Hywel Sele, who lived in Nannau at the time, tried to kill him. Unfortunately for Hywel, Owain always wore plates of iron under his clothes. Owain promptly killed Hywel Sele and threw his body into a nearby hollow tree trunk. The body was not found for another forty years and the tree was from then on called 'Ceubren yr Ellyll' ('The Demon's Hollow Tree').

Another famous man from Nannau was the poet Llywelyn Goch ab Meurig Hen (1350-90), who wrote one of the finest love-poems in Welsh: 'Marwnad Lleucu Llwyd' ('The Death of Lleucu Llwyd'). Lleucu was a beautiful young woman from Pennal who happened to be in love with Llywelyn. Her father, however, did not approve of her choice in the least. He decided to tell Lleucu that Llywelyn had married another woman, hoping that she would then forget about him. But her father hadn't realised the strength of her feelings for her sweetheart; as soon as Lleucu heard her father's words, she fell to the floor in shock and died, heartbroken. When Llywelyn heard of her death, he wrote his passionate, extremely moving poem.

Yes, there's wealth of romance and history in the area, and Cader Idris itself is full of romance and magic, from the strange light on Geugraig when the sun strikes the white stones in the fissures, to the Arthurian mists rising from the lakes of Cregennen at the foot of Y Tyrrau Mawr. You've probably heard the legend about spending the night on Cader: when you wake, the following morning, you will be a poet, completely mad or dead. If you wake at all, that is. That's probably why the mountain has attracted some very strange people over the years. One of the wardens told me that he once met a very old, hippy-like man on the summit. He asked him whether he came here often. 'Yes,' he replied, 'I've been coming here for two thousand years.' You may laugh, but somehow, when you're standing on the summit with the mists and winds howling around you, or lying in the grass by Cregennen, watching the sun set over Cardigan Bay, it's not that difficult to believe that old man's words.

On This Mountain

# THE BLORENGE
## John Barnie

If you lived on our side of Abergavenny, the Blorenge was the hill you climbed least. To get to it you either had to take a bus to Llanfoist or walk two miles through town, across the Castle Meadows and over the Merthyr Road bridge to the village, before you even began. Much easier to climb the foothills of the Black Mountains – the Deri or Rholben – that gave access to the Sugar Loaf; or Bryn Arw, or the Big or Little Skirrid.

Even so, it was the Blorenge you were most aware of, a dark bulwark lowering over the town, glimpsed even from the narrow main street above rooftops. On summer evenings from our garden you could watch the sun set over its ridge, the turquoise sky barred with clouds like a mirror image of a ribbed watery beach, Venus glittering above the mountain as the sun sharpened the rim to a black, irregular blade.

At night, if the cloud was low and thick, its underside would be disturbed far across the Blorenge by a restless orange glare, a reflection from the blast furnaces at Ebbw Vale. I used to imagine the great cauldrons of molten, glowing metal, the smoke and clanking and shouts in the giant works, whose products passed our house every day in the form of bars and sheets and rods of steel on the flatbeds of British Road Services lorries.

In winter when snow fell, the slopes of the mountain gleamed like white spinnakers. Then it was dangerous for the BRS lorries inching down Blackrock, before the Heads of the Valleys dual carriageway was built. There were reports sometimes of a lorry going over the edge into Clydach gorge or crashing into the Rock itself. On the slope of the Hereford Road just above our house, a dozen or more flatbeds with tons of fresh steel might get stuck in the icy conditions and women would run out with bucketsfull of cinders and ash to scatter under the wheels.

Unlike the other hills surrounding the town, the Blorenge was always associated with industry; its great scarp a frontier between the Usk valley and the industrial valleys to the west. It was a permeable frontier, though. In the 1960s, I met an old man from Govilon who in his childhood could remember miners living in the village who climbed the mountain every day to work in the coal mines beyond; then after a long shift they descended the Blorenge's eighteen hundred feet home again. That was before the First World War.

The Monmouthshire and Brecon Canal that follows a contour line at the foot of the mountain is also deeply involved in its industrial past, built to carry, among other things, coal and iron from Blaenafon to Newport. When I knew it, though, this could hardly be guessed at as large stretches of the canal were derelict, with surviving reaches such as the one between Gilwern and Llanfoist deserted, except for the splash of oars in summer when boaters hired Edwardian skiffs at Gilwern. It was a good place to take a girlfriend, the skiff cleaving the still brown water where, leaning over, you could make a window out of your shadow and watch stands of Canadian pondweed drift by, or shoals of roach with brown backs and red fins, streaking off to the side away from the smooth progression of the boat. There were kingfishers as well, and sometimes herons; and all the while, the overhang of branches from the woods on the Blorenge's lower slopes, and the sense of the mountain's weight and bulk invisible above you.

If you were used to the shambling hogbacks of the Black Mountains, climbing the Blorenge was a surprise. Instead of a narrow ridge and a steep descent the other side, you were faced by acres of uneven moorland comprised of hummocky stands of heather and whin that stretched on and on. Walking there it was impossible not to be aware that the moor is littered with ruins. The Black Mountains have their ruins too; upland farmsteads and byres abandoned in the nineteenth century, the roofs and walls long since collapsed into piles of lichened stones. But on the Blorenge the scale is different. There are tumbled piles of waste from the limestone quarries that scar its surface; grassed-over remains of tramways that in the early nineteenth century criss-crossed the moor, transporting limestone to the ironworks at Blaenafon and down the hillside to the lime kilns at Govilon and Llanfoist. A tramroad ran, too, from Blaenafon ironworks to the forge at Garn-ddyrys where pig iron was turned into wrought iron. The slag heaps at Garn-ddyrys teeter on the side of the mountain, stained brown, red and yellow, like aberrant outcrops or lesions in the body of the rock. The grassy bed of the tramway rises gently in the direction of Blaenafon, passing the dam at Pen-ffordd-goch, constructed in 1824 to supply water to the Garn-ddyrys forge. The water of the dam presents a placid surface to the sky, but nothing seems to grow there, not even algae on its stone-covered depths.

In places where the topsoil has collapsed at Garn-ddyrys, the substrate is black with coal grit, while elsewhere spoil heaps from early coal mining are yet to be colonised by vegetation. They are a reminder that, although when viewed from Abergavenny, the Blorenge doesn't look so different from the Black Mountains, its geology is in fact very different. The Sugar Loaf is composed of old red sandstone capped with

The Blorenge

millstone grit; the Blorenge, on the outer edge of the coalfield, has beds of carboniferous limestone, ironstone, and seams of coal, the combination which gave the area a unique advantage at the beginning of the industrial revolution. The entry for Abergavenny in *The Universal British Directory* of 1793 notes that the town's environs 'are rich and beautiful, and, like the rest of the vale from Brecknock, abound with the most charming variety of landscape,' adding that 'The prospects are terminated at proper distances with mountains, among which, at the opposite side of the town, Skirid-vawr and Blorench raise their conspicuous heads.' This is from the great age of the gentleman traveller in search of the 'Sublime', but, the *Directory* continues, 'The mountains in this neighbourhood abound with iron ore, coal, and lime; and theron have been lately erected, at a very great expence, the following capital iron works, viz. Blanavon, by Thomas Hill, Esq. and Co. Beaufort, by Edward Kendall, Esq. Sirhowy, by Thomas Atkinson, Esq. and Co. and Ebber Vale, by Jere Homfrey, Esq. and Co.' The entry is a reminder that in 1793 the aesthetics of the Romantic movement that valued mountain 'prospects' went hand in hand with the industrial revolution, and entrepreneurs who looked at the same mountains with very different prospects in view.

A few years after the *Universal British Directory* was published, the Blorenge was transformed. Whole villages sprang up, like the one at Pwll-du for the men who worked Walter Lewis's limestone quarry. At its height the quarry supplied limestone to the kilns at the foot of the Blorenge as well as to Thomas Hill, Esq.'s ironworks in Blaenafon. Pwll-du had housing for workers and a manager, as well as a pub, a school, stables and a store run by the Blaenavon Company. When the quarry ceased operations, though, the village lost its raison d'être; its remains were eventually demolished in the twentieth century and next to nothing of it survives.

Walk the Blorenge now and its moor can seem a monument to the fleeting nature of our ambitions and dreams, a palimpsest where human activity has come and gone since at least the Bronze Age when people built barrows for the dead there. Slowly nature is reasserting itself over the industrial plundering of the nineteenth century. Limestone cliffs in some of the quarries are home to the whitebeam, a rare deciduous tree; pools associated with the workings are now important breeding grounds for dragonflies; even the red grouse, an increasingly rare species in Wales, manages to hang on in the heather and whin, long after the ironmasters' gamekeepers have gone.

Human activity on the Blorenge continues, though, echoing the preoccupations of our own tamed, post-industrial age. Against the retaining wall of the Pen-ffordd-goch dam – better known now as Keeper's Pond after the gamekeepers who

The Blorenge

once patrolled the moor – there is a tarmacked car park where people come to walk their dogs, skirting the rim of the Blorenge to admire the view of the Usk valley below and the rolling prospect of the Black Mountains crowned by the Sugar Loaf, set off at a 'proper distance', as the author of the *Universal British Directory* would say. At appropriate venues on the moor, information points tell you what you ought to be looking at. As your car climbs beyond the Fiddler's Elbow on the road to Blaenafon, you pass the 'Cordell Country Inn', its name changed from The Royal Oak. For some years historians and archaeologists have been unpacking the complex history of early industrialisation in Monmouthshire and the Blorenge's role in it, but the short, brutish assault of the ironmasters and quarry owners on the mountain is filtered for most visitors through the Tourist Board's account of it.

Today the Blorenge is owned by the South-East Wales Hang Gliding and Paragliding Club, and when the weather is right you can watch from Abergavenny as the multi-coloured hang gliders, like gaudy figures out of a *Spiderman* comic, whirl slowly down to land in the Castle Meadows.

Human notions of ownership are illusory, however. Except for their cairns, the people of the Bronze Age have vanished without trace; the flurry and noise of the forges and mines and quarries have been stilled across the moor and on the mountain's flanks. The Blorenge was there thirty thousand years ago when a glacier scoured the Usk valley below, and tributary glaciers disgorged into it from the hanging valleys of St David's and St Mary's Vales, in the the Black Mountains beyond. Wind, frost and rain continue their work, diminishing the slag heaps at Garn-ddyrys; lichen, upland grass, heather and whin encroach on the stones. Seen from the mountain's perspective, the hang gliders are ephemeral as butterflies, owning nothing but the summer's day.

The Blorenge

On This Mountain

The Blorenge

On This Mountain

# ON THE BLACK RIDGE
## Jim Perrin

To see the ghostly outline of an old landscape beneath the superficial covering of the contemporary . . .

Simon Schama, *Landscape and Memory*

We – being the photographer Ray Wood and myself – are sitting in Caban, Brynrefail's excellent café which is the jealously guarded secret of the North Wales outdoor community, whose members are happy to surrender to the weekend visitor all the delights of Pete's Eats in Llanberis so long as their favoured haunt remains civilized, chip-free and relatively uncrowded. It is difficult these days to find anywhere not thronging with weekend visitors in Snowdonia, so you can see their point in wishing to retain Caban as a village amenity. Though for myself, I've never much liked this principle of exclusivity, and would rather take my chance in the ebb and flow of the human tide. There are always places for exercise or for relaxation or contemplation where you can go to avoid the crowds, and Caban for the moment is one of them. I'll tell you about that name later, because it has a history, a *frisson*, a connection into what I want to talk about here. But first I want to give you a thought from a volume of autobiographical reminiscence by the Welsh poet and scholar

W.J. Gruffydd, a quarryman's son who was born and lived his early life in a neighbouring village to Brynrefail, in the northerly foothills between Snowdon and the sea. He's a writer to whom I feel considerable temperamental affinity, his work imbued with a sense of place and regional culture all too often disregarded or dismissed by the casual visitor and the modish outdoor *litterateur*. As here, for example (in translation from the Welsh), from the chapter 'Nant yr Wyddfa' that begins *Hen Atgofion: Blynyddoedd y Locust*:

I set out by car from Cardiff at nightfall, and, after driving through lashing rain and wind all the way, I reached Nant yr Wyddfa [the old local name for the Pass of Llanberis between Gorffwysfa and Penllyn by Brynrefail] about two o'clock in the morning. For a moment the black clouds had dispersed, and the vast majesty of the Snowdon crags shimmered beneath the unnumbered stars. I stopped the car and got out.

Cefn Du

Suddenly in a flash of perception, I realized that the criticism of malignant and ignorant people is less than dust on the scales – something too insignificant even to be amusing. I was given five minutes – perhaps it was only five seconds – of assurance, of personal freedom from petty things; in the stillness of those minutes between Snowdon and the Glyderau I *saw* how my whole life, through having been too often a prey to fools, had lost all serenity and tranquillity. I do not think I shall ever again be tormented by anything as petty as prejudice . . . my mind turns more and more to the old things and the old folk. The truth is that I have never lived in a community since I left Llanddeiniolen for Cardiff a quarter of a century ago. Here I simply reside – sleeping, working and eating. I do not *live* here.

This heartfelt memoir of a time past was written for an express purpose which Gruffydd makes clear in another redolent passage, that chimes closely with my purpose:

Sometimes, in my bed when I cannot sleep, I bring to mind the homes of my native place, and I repeat the name of everyone who lived in each of them in my time or the time of my parents; and after dropping off to sleep, I dream of the old people who have gone: my father and mother, my grandfather and my grandmother, my aunt Elin Huws of Cae Meta, Dafydd and Lewis Huws . . .

I look for the latter name on the map as Ray and I sit over our coffee, and find it there on a gentle southerly slope above the Afon Seiont, old woodland and an old settlement behind, the people of the place from W.J. Gruffydd's time long gone. He continues:

. . . for a moment on waking, I feel overwhelming happiness because I can still have their company. I don't know what Freud or Jung would say about this, and I don't care. I shall now prolong by a little the allotted period of the old community by writing the story of those times.

Well, where did all this matter go? Other plays in the repertory have been performed here since, though the backdrop – Snowdon, the Glyderau, rivers and woods – has remained constant, changes in it no more than ones of detail and use. This scene has been important in my life. For years I lived and worked in a house – when I sold it, it was to Ray Wood – the windows of which looked out across Llyn Padarn

On This Mountain

to Cefn Du. My son Will grew up here. The woods and rocks and hills were his playground. On my kitchen wall in Dyffryn Tanat now hangs a large oil painting of that dark ridge opposite: Cefn Du, the black ridge . . .

So here in Caban, Ray and I are squandering the day, shrinking away from the glower of it and the grey clouds. It is All Souls' Night, and this vision of a hill has come to possess me. Cefn Du – few come here, and those who do mostly arrive by the tarmac road that approaches within a quarter-mile of its Ordnance Survey pillar. In every other quarter of Eryri these hills teem with folk, the more with every passing year – but not this one, not this sombre, atmospheric height

between Gwyrfai and Seiont. I muse on that, remember its moods – the imperial blush of august heather, winter's snowy ermine, its solidity against the fleet scud of cloud – and envision it as an ambiguous place:

> . . . where the damned have howled away their hearts,
>   And where the blessed dance.

Ray and I drive round to the path which broaches the ridge from the north-west, intending to traverse the hill back to the house where he now lives on Water Street in Llanberis. We climb past pylons and under power-lines that hiss and crackle at the mist, navigate through a web of stone-walled fields by gated, rocky ways, past mounds of burnt stones and the outlines of hut-circles that pre-date any written history, and are debouched finally on to the moor, which is dense and heathery and dark. This is the secret of this place – this is its notation, the key in which it resonates. This is what sets it apart, makes it special, ensures that it be left unvisited. You can acquire your summits, tread your peaks, scramble along your ridges, rattle down your screes. But a moor takes away all your definitives, leaves you errant and unsure. Its vagueness teases at Ray's map as he tries to orient himself, and moor's perpetual ally the wind colludes to flap it away. Its heather smothers and obliterates all semblance of paths, however optimistically they are marked down on paper. Listen to this, by the Scottish writer Nan Shepherd, whose book about the Cairngorms, *The Living Mountain*, for the natural quality of this unfeted woman's writing, for her unselfconscious 'eco-consciousness' and the simple, heartfelt subtleties of her expression, is the finest-ever piece of writing about British landscape. This passage is not from that neglected masterpiece – though it gives a sense of its quality – but from her novel of 1954, *A Pass in the Grampians*:

> For the sheep farmer, seventy years of intercourse had made the moor sit to him more closely than the most supple of garments . . . He had made his covenant with the moor: it had bogged him and drenched him, deceived, scorched, numbed him with cold, tested his endurance, memory and skill; until a large part of his nature was so interpenetrated with its nature that apart from it he would have lost reality. His love for it indeed was beyond all covenant. Like his love for Jenny, it had the quality of life itself, absolute and uncovenanted.

Ray and I, we do not *live* here, have only looked on at it for years in all its changing moods and seasons, from behind glass and a near distance. We flounder; we follow faint leads through squelching, heavy ground; we chaff good-naturedly at each other's ignorance and incompetence; we crest the ridge and are battered in the wind's wuther and blast; we look out over Caernarfon Bay, all dappled mercury and pewter, and watch the white horses chasing over Caernarfon Bar; we see the squalls drift towards us as shimmering columns across the

flats of Anglesey northerly; we prepare for our drenching. Before rain and hail reach us, we have slipped inside the draughty roofless ruin of Marconi's 1914 wireless station, from which the first direct radio message was sent across the Atlantic that year, and four years later to Australia. Ghosts of electricity are howling on the storm as we cower in the shell of the building and huddle into our waterproofs. That pathless mile, steep and stumbling, through the heather has eaten up the remnants of the day. Dark falls. We venture out into gale and hiss of hail to make our Hallowe'en descent through the deserted workings of the Glynrhonwy quarries. I remember Thomas Pennant's description of descending Snowdon in a storm: 'The prospect down was horrible. It gave an idea of numbers of abysses, concealed by thick smoke, furiously circulating around us. Very often a gust of wind formed an opening in the clouds, which gave a fine distinct vista of lake and valley'. The streetlights of Llanberis make our treacherous foreground of slate-tip and quarry-hole all the more opaque. From the lunar primitive of the moor, out of the skeletal remnants of technology's genesis, down through post-industrial desolation where whistle of the wind and the slip of settling spoil clacks out our sole accompaniment, we descend to connect into glimmering narrow ways whose scraped stones struck sparks from the hobnails of the quarrymen – W.J. Gruffydd's father among them, no doubt – so few decades ago in these hills' scheme of things. I find myself invoking that

Cefn Du

On This Mountain

word *caban* as I clatter down in the unlight. It was the term used for the bleak slate huts where the quarrymen took their breaks, sheltered when necessary from the extremes of mountain weather. But it stood also as symbol for the autodidactic intensity of those former working communities, unconnected with the new world, concerned to explore and evaluate and learn, to perpetuate and amplify their own culture, to reject the merely meretricious and resist depredation and corruption.

In the dark, threading down by tenuous links, we come into the new, neon, weekend-and-holiday sensation-seeking world of Llanberis, and I walk down Goodman Street with a stanza of the old Welsh scholar-poet Gruffydd echoing distantly – *'Mor fyr llawenydd. Nid oes go'/Ond cochni'r maes lle troedient gynt,/A gwywder lle bu'r llwyfan dro,/A darnau papur yn y gwynt./Mae'r pasiant trosodd; fe aeth Wil/I lawr y glyn . . .'* – which translates like this:

> How short is joy. Nothing remains in memory
> But the red of the field where once they walked,
> And the faded light of the former stage,
> And scraps of paper on the wind.
> The pageant is over; Will went
>   Down the valley . . .

(For Will Perrin, 1980-2004, who felt deeply and despaired of the world.)

Cefn Du

On This Mountain

# DINAS BRÂN, LLANGOLLEN
## Jane MacNamee

This is the secret of the land…you can only watch it escaping away from you…Its past is its future, for it lives by memories and in advance it recedes. The greatest of its heroes have no graves, for they will come again. Indeed they have not died; they have only disappeared.

John Cowper Powys

This entry appears in the diary John Cowper Powys kept, whilst writing his haunting novel on the rise and fall of Wales's most celebrated and enigmatic hero, 'Owen Glendower'. Set in part on Castell Dinas Brân, a friend lends me a copy for some 'quirky association' before our walk to Hyddgen, mid-Wales, the site of one of Glyn Dŵr's greatest victories. We set out under the enchanting fizz of a November sky, a faltering drizzle falling on the soft flanks of Pumlumon. Just beyond a footbridge at the confluence of Afon Hyddgen and Afon Hengwm, two white quartz stones glint out of a thick matting of auburn bracken. These are the *Cerrig Cyfamod Owain Glyn Dŵr* ('The Covenant Stones of Owain Glyn Dŵr'), solemn promises made to a continued enterprise, after a seemingly impossible victory, a 'point-of-no-return'.

A month later, I carry the vision of that battlefield and Cowper Powys's novel with me on my way to Dinas Brân,
driving deep into Glyn Dŵr territory, passing Corwen and Glyndyfrdwy, curling through the shifting mists of the Dee Valley, the rioting waters of the river below, and on into Llangollen. Parked up, I amble through town past the war memorial flashed red with poppy wreaths tattered by a month of unrelenting rain, and jarring with the scarlet fleecy Santa cap of a passing Christmas shopper. I linger over coffee in a café full of pine, tinsel and steam, to read the opening pages of the book again.

Over these last few weeks, I have fallen under the spell of Powys's mesmeric prose, allured by the character of Rhisiart ap Owen, Glyn Dŵr's cousin and secretary. The novel begins on the Eve of St John 1400, with the intense and youthful Rhisiart, an Oxford scholar, returning to his ancestral routes to present himself to Glyn Dŵr, in a country on the brink of bloody revolt. On his way to meet Owain at Glyndyfrdwy, he will pass by the ruins of Castell Dinas Brân, where his 'traitor-ancestor' died. Approaching it, he is gripped with nervous anticipation at the prospect of seeing, for the first time, the magnificent castle he has built in his mind since he was a boy. That castle was once the 13th-century seat of Gruffudd ap Madog, its original splendour a symbol of a prince at the height of his power. On his death it fell into the unruly hands of his four sons, the Princes of Powys Fadog, whose conflicting and switching allegiances between the English crown and Llywelyn, then recognized as the Prince of all Wales, ensured its downfall. Threatened with an invasion by Henry de Lacy, Earl of Lincoln in May 1277, its defenders decided to burn it down themselves, rather than have it fall into the hands of the English or of Welsh traitors. Although there was enough left to warrant its reconstruction, it was overlooked as too remote, and finally abandoned as a ruin, following one more struggle for possession between Dafydd ap Gruffudd and the English invaders of the 1280s.

Dinas Brân may not have played a historical part in Glyn Dŵr's campaigns, but it caught Cowper Powys's imagination enough for him to bring it into the heart of the novel. For Rhisiart, it symbolised 'the mystic terminus of every vista of his imagination'. He is so moved on its first sighting, he falls to his knees in supplication:

. . . it took into itself that whole hill it was built upon! Yes, that was the thing . . . not the stones of its human walls, not the majestic outlines of its towering battlements, not its soaring arches and turrets and bastions; it was an impregnable mountain called up out of that deep valley by some supernatural mandate. Its foundations were sunk in the earth, but they were sunk in more than the earth; they were sunk in that mysterious underworld of beyond-reality whence rises the eternal archetypes of all the refuges and all the sanctuaries of the spirit, untouched by time, inviolable ramparts not built by hands!

Not surprisingly I approach with both excitement and a tint of fear – how will the contemporary jolt with Rhisiart's 'ideal of perfection'? My first contact could not be more incongruous. I head towards the ramparts from the west, walking up from Llangollen bridge, past the taxidermists' in the sheeting rain. No-one else is bothering, apart from a group of mud-splattered mountain bikers shooting past me before striking out along the canal. I'm not sure who looks more ridiculous – they, pedalling the crazy gradient like giant insects in their black lycra suits, or me, choosing a day like this. The bikers gone onto a more solid, level route, I turn onto the start of the footpath, under a pewter sky.

Dinas Brân

On This Mountain

A wooden signpost directs me through a caged walkway by the Science and Arts building of the local school, steel fence posts like corrugated spears on one side and a stream to my right. A thin flow of water chokes downwards on its journey through piles of discarded plastic fruit-juice cartons, Yo-yo biscuit wrappers, scarlet packets of Trident mints, Grolsch bottles, empty cartons of Marlboro and Rothmans, crushed cola cans, and sodden dog faeces knotted in transparent pastel-pink bags, wedged downstream into the green hatch of plastic fencing that billows out onto my path.

My skin bristling and chuntering to myself about the indestructible, inexcusable waste of the modern age, I glimpse the castle high up ahead, and push on through the detritus, past a fencepost scrawled with the word 'ORDER' in blue pen, until something rustles out to greet me from the scrub. A mistle thrush, one of my favourite birds, lofts out of the rubbish and perches on the barbed-wire fencing, pushing out his proud dappled breast, eyeing me closely. I stand still whilst he considers our positions, before hurrying off again, urgent in his winter gatherings. Invigorated by the artistry of his wings, I take heed. He, unlike me, will not be disappointed by the impossible romance of anything. He is just surviving, as is, of course, the ruin of Castell Dinas Brân, still fully of itself,

inspite of the plastic, the rain, its continuing decay, and whatever I might imagine it to be.

Through a kissing gate, the rising path is lined with bare hedges of hazel, a few straggling leaves still clinging to autumn with withering stems, and long spikes of hawthorn bejewelled by the rain, hanging heavy. Beyond the hedges, soft lights from two or three houses glow through the cloud, the homes of more sensible folk wrapped warm and dry inside, the delicious smell of wood smoke licking out of the chimneys, twining with the mist. I am so tempted to knock.

I resist and continue steeply upwards, squelching through the juicy copper rot of oak and blackened rowan leaves, and out onto the lower slopes of the hill. Defining its contours, thick emerald garlands of moss spiral upwards layer upon layer as if around an ancient mystic head, the ruined battlements perched on its skull at some lunatic angle – at once the battered crown of a defeated prince, and a jaw ripped out of the shale.

Halfway up, I pause to look back down over Llangollen. It is as if the whole valley and its surrounding hills are breathing out. The giant tent of the International Eisteddfod, an upturned conch, ear close to the pulse of ground, gleams white through the steam of the railway. As the train pulls through the valley it tugs chimney smoke and swirling vapours rising from the treetops with it, before letting out a slow high-pitched wail. A single piercing note reverberates off the bleak rock, echoing from every ridge, and underneath it, the whoosh of the traffic, the whirr of an ambulance siren, and the distant hammering of metal.

As I reach the crown and step into the ramparts, an eerie silence negates all sound from the valley floor. Pressing my hand to the jagged edges of the fallen masonry, feeling the whole history of the castle and its prehistoric hill fort converge in the decay of its majestic arches, I touch, unnervingly, on Rhisiart's 'supernatural mandate'. Moving inwards, I stand on what looks like a giant shield of moss, irridescent at the heart of the siltstone remains, and feel it again, that 'something other' Rhisiart describes during his fictional incarceration here. It is:

> . . . in some extraordinary manner not as solidly material
> as other places. And why shouldn't there be spots like this
> on the surface of the earth where the electric currents of
> good and evil have clashed and contended for so long
> that they have drawn the opacity out of 'matter'?

It is as if the ruin is suspended in a timeless void, a living chamber of memories for centuries of human struggle,

absorbing the vital force of the hill beneath it, the cinnamon larches and the dusky mauve branches of silver birch leaning hard into it. Through the mercurial cloud I watch the surrounding landscape escaping from me – the graceful line of the Berwyn, Llantysilio mountain to the north, the lilac-banded scarp of Eglwyseg, and far off to the east, the plains of Shropshire. I am entranced by those fleeting visions, reminded of all the transitory I cannot grasp, and my absurd human ache for certainty. Perplexed and slightly uneasy, the downward path dissolving in the mist and the rain coming in again, I flash back to the words in Cowper Powys's diary – to heroes without graves and their returning. One word seems to whisper serpentine around the battlements, 'Difancoll' – Disappearance? Oblivion? Both? Which? I decide not to stay up here too long.

'Difancoll' is the title of Powys's final chapter in which, in a bold creative leap of historical inaccuracy, he has Glyn Dŵr cremated on the nearby summit of Mynydd-y-Gaer. It was here that Powys came on Christmas Eve 1939 to write the last lines of his novel on hearing of the tragic death of his most beloved brother, Llywelyn, and following news of the outbreak of World War Two. He ends with Owain's son, Meredith, leaving the burning remains of his father and descending from the mountain towards Carrog in the grey dawn light, not

Dinas Brân

On This Mountain

defeated by his death, but comforted by the sight first, of a magnificently-horned stag, and then two soaring ravens croaking eastwards, '. . . the visions of thousands of generations of men living in these hills . . . Something stores them up; a spirit that is more than just ourselves.'

Soaked through with ghosts, I take comfort too in the 'stored up' spirit of a shimmering crow I meet on my descent, lording it over the dead trunk of an oak. Messenger, opportunist, pragmatist, he dances yobbishly about, scouting out for his next carcass. And when he finds it, everything will be consumed, nothing will be wasted. He will pick the bones clean and they will crumble back into the ground in the endless cycle. In the spring, scabious and harebell will prickle out new shoots through the rot, and fresh velvetine ferns will uncurl their secrets in questioning fronds.

Dinas Brân

On This Mountain

# Y BERWYN
## Iolo Williams

To the majority of people who travel from mid to north Wales and back, the Berwyn Mountains are a brown wilderness full of heather, sheep and very little else. But to me, they are a paradise of tranquillity, wildlife and old friends.

They are called the Berwyn Mountains, but in reality, they are little more than hills. Despite the fact that Cadair Berwyn and Moel Sych, the two highest peaks, rise to over two thousand feet, they are part of a range of hills that extend from Bala in the north to Y Foel in the south and eastwards as far as Llangollen. Despite their lack of altitude, they have never suffered an inferiority complex because their unique character ensures that they can compete with any mountain range, anywhere in the world.

I was brought up in the shadow of these mountains, in the small village of Llanwddyn. It was an idyllic childhood, playing in the woods and fishing with friends, all part of a tight-knit community. I couldn't have asked for a better childhood, or a more friendly and welcoming village, but as I look back today, perhaps the greatest legacy the area gave me was my love for wildlife and the environment.

I began to wander the hills at a very young age with our dog, Bitw, and although I spent many a long day traversing the moors, my mum and dad never worried about me. I would virtually live on these moors in the spring and summer, eating trout from upland lakes, plants, seeds and fruits from the forests and drinking cold, clear water from mountain streams before returning home to a nice, warm bed. Indeed there were many occasions when I was walking the hills when I should have been in school, but searching for nesting birds in the open air was far more important to a young schoolboy than chemistry or maths lessons in a stuffy classroom.

My most memorable days up on the Berwyn were those when I was asked to survey breeding birds for the RSPB. These were the days before Health and Safety ruled our lives and I was allowed to wander at will, armed only with a map and pencil to mark my observations. There were no mobile phones nor rucksacks laden with safety equipment, just a raincoat, binoculars and plenty of common sense. I would often spend several days at a time up on the hills, before hunger and fatigue drove me back down to civilization.

On a calm, spring morning, I would set off for the moors in the early hours, long before daybreak, with only the occasional tawny owl to keep me company as I wandered through the tall, dark coniferous woodlands that encircle the Berwyn. Once out on the open hill, only silence and the odd gust of wind kept me company but, as first light approached, the upland birds began to awaken.

The first birds to call are the black grouse. Every spring, the males gather at traditional sites called 'leks' where they display every dawn and dusk to attract a mate. The males, or blackcock, are stunning birds, about the size of a small turkey, with blue-black feathers, a white lyre-shaped tail and bright red wattles above the eyes. Watching half a dozen or more displaying at dawn is a magical sight, a bit like watching a disco but it's the males rather than the females who gather around their handbags and strut their funky stuff.

When a female does venture out from the safety of the surrounding heather onto the 'lek', all hell is let loose as each male does his utmost to impress the visiting greyhen. In reality, it is the dominant male at the centre of the display ground that mates with around 80% of the females, but it's important for the younger males to work out a hierarchy for future years. After mating, the females fly off to lay their eggs and rear the young , leaving the males to impress the next visitor to their 'lek'.

The Berwyn moors provide the best place in southern Britain to see black grouse and although the population declined dramatically during the 1980s and 1990s, the latest counts show that on these and some adjacent uplands, this unique bird is once more beginning to reclaim lost ground.

Other birds display at first light too. Over some of the bogs, the bubbling call of the curlew is an integral part of spring and the horse-like neighing of displaying snipe can be heard each morning and evening. The noise is actually made by the two outermost tail feathers as the bird dives earthwards. As the light strengthens, the display stops and the pair will eventually lay three or four eggs in a tuft of grass among the wetter parts of the moorland. The curlew will also look to areas of tall vegetation to lay her superbly camouflaged, mottled brown eggs.

Once the sun has broken the horizon and warmed the air, the birds of prey awake. Buzzards are often the first ones to be seen and although they nest in the tall trees around the periphery of the hills, they venture out over the moor to hunt. Like the raven, they will take advantage of any sheep unlucky enough to die out on the hill, but they also hunt rabbits and voles that seek refuge amongst the heather and bracken. The small mammals also attract the kestrel, or windhover. As its old

Y Berwyn

On This Mountain

English name suggests, it is often to be seen hovering above unwary prey before folding its wings and plummeting to ground, its murderous talons outstretched. The male, with its grey head and tail, and its orange-brown back is my father's favourite bird, and the son too enjoys watching this aerial acrobat using the sky like a playground.

My favourite bird, however, is the hen harrier and the Berwyn hills are one of its British strongholds. I remember finding a pair on the moors above Llanwddyn when I was eleven years old, and dancing my way down from the mountain as if I'd been selected to play full-back for Wales. Ever since that day, I have been captivated by these birds and you'll find nowhere better to watch them than an isolated moorland valley on the Berwyn at the beginning of summer.

They spend the winter months in the lowlands but when April brings its warmer weather, the birds return to their traditional upland breeding grounds. The ghostly, grey-blue male returns first and in order to attract a mate, he performs a stunning 'roller-coaster' display flight over the dark heather. Once, on a warm, sunny morning in an isolated valley in the heart of the Berwyn moors, I watched three males displaying together, a sight that remains vivid in the memory as I write. Their pale colour stands out against the dark brown heather and soon, they will have been joined by the drab female as the nesting season begins in earnest.

Even when one is lying amongst the heather around noon, and most birds are having a short 'siesta', there is still plenty to see. Common lizards sunbathe on patches of acid grassland before scurrying towards cover at the merest hint of danger and field voles dash from one tuft of grass to the next beneath my feet. These two are an important food source, not only for many upland birds of prey, but also for mammals such as foxes, stoats and weasels.

Periodically, large grey moths with huge 'eyes' on each wing will fly past at great speed. These are emperor moths, the day-flying males hurrying along the pheromone scent trails laid down by the females. The large 'eyes' are reputed to scare off would-be predators but I often find the remains of these moths scattered all over the hill, no doubt eaten by the agile merlin or even a passing hobby.

Sundew thrive in the very wet areas. This is a plant which

has adapted well to such a barren environment as some of the leaves secrete a special glue to catch passing insects. The sundew then sucks the liquid from the insect's body, these added nutrients allowing it to thrive in such a hostile environment.

The Berwyn moors are also a stronghold for our smallest falcon, the dashing little merlin. Over the winter months, it follows its chief prey, small birds, down to the lowland estuaries and marshes before returning, like the hen harrier, to the uplands in spring. It's a difficult bird to see because it hunts by flying rapidly just inches above the heather, but a pair together is very noisy indeed and on a still moorland, their frenetic calls can be heard for over two kilometres.

I would stay on the hill from before first light until dark, and as the sun began to set, the short-eared owl would emerge from its daytime roost. This is Wales's rarest owl and even in perfect habitat like the Berwyn moors, it is rarely seen. It's a buoyant, long-winged bird and it flies like a large, yellow-brown tern, low over the ground as it hunts for voles or the occasional inexperienced nestling, fresh out of the nest.

Like many upland birds, it nests on the floor amongst tall vegetation. The female lays up to eight white, round eggs, but it is so well hidden that only when I've almost trodden on the sitting female have I ever seen one. In years when vole numbers are particularly high, more than half a dozen pairs nest on the hill but many a summer passed without my seeing a single bird.

I'm sure many of you believe that it is impossible to see so much incredible wildlife in one day but this is what makes the Berwyn such a special place. Days like this were my bread and butter for so many springs and summers, and recording all the natural wonders would have taken several volumes.

In addition to the wildlife, I never cease to be drawn in by the landscape of this unique area in the heart of Wales. Some sites such as Pistyll Rhaeadr, the tallest waterfall in Wales, are well known and well visited, but I prefer to look for the quieter nooks and crannies well off the beaten track.

On a cold, snowy winter's day, nothing beats a walk along the Berwyn ridge as far as Moel Sych and Cadair Berwyn. Here, I have seen a stoat in its pure white ermine coat, and a grey squirrel, over a mile from the nearest tree! In August, a drive along the road between Llangynog and Y Bala is a colourful experience with the mauves of the heather and the yellow gorse competing with the sweet scent as it wafts in through the car window. I can think of nowhere more spectacular to be buried than the churchyard of Pennant Melangell, surrounded by steep hills, deciduous woodland and heather moor, and the views looking down from the Lake Vyrnwy hotel are among the best, and most famous, in Britain. It's no wonder that several Hollywood stars have taken advantage of the hotel's warm welcome.

But for me, what makes Berwyn so much more special is its people. I recall giving up a day's bird counting to help an old farmer gather his sheep on the hills above Llandderfel. We chatted as we worked and he explained that he loved nothing better than to walk the hills with his dog, and he could name every nesting bird along the northern edge of the moor. As the sun shone on our backs, I looked up to see a red kite circling

RSPB **What's about**

Species Seen Regularly + J

| | | |
|---|---|---|
| GREAT TIT | GREEN WOODPECKER | SPOTTED FLYCATCHER |
| BLUE TIT | G.S. WOODPECKER | HOUSE MARTIN |
| COAL TIT | TREECREEPER | SWALLOW |
| MARSH TIT | RAVEN | SWIFT |
| WILLOW TIT | JACKDAW | TREE PIPIT |
| LONG TAILED TIT | CARRION CROW | REDPOLL |
| NUTHATCH | STOCK DOVE | REDSTART |
| CHAFFINCH | ROBIN | PIED FLYCATCHER |
| GREENFINCH | WREN | BLACKCAP |
| GOLDFINCH | CROSSBILL | CUCKOO |
| BULLFINCH | SISKIN | WOOD WARBLER |
| PHEASANT | GREY WAGTAIL | SEDGE WARBLER |
| REEVES PHEASANT | PIED WAGTAIL | COMMON WHITETHROAT |
| | GARDEN WARBLER | RED KITE |
| WOODPIGEON | | MORE INFO ON REVERSE |
| SPARROWHAWK | LINNET | |
| GOSHAWK | JAY | COMMON SANDPIPER |
| PEREGRINE | HOUSE SPARROW | MALLARD |
| HEN HARRIER | MEADOW PIPIT | GOOSANDER |
| | SKYLARK | G.C. GREBE |
| BUZZARD | MAGPIE | CORMORANT |
| TAWNY OWL | GOLD CREST | GREY HERON |
| THRUSH | DUNNOCK | KINGFISHER |
| | CHIFFCHAFF | DIPPER |

On This Mountain

overhead – the first I had ever seen on these hills. The hours flew by and at the end of a long day, we retreated to a nearby pub for a meal and a pint of cold beer. The perfect end to a memorable day.

I still live within a short distance of this unique place and even today, with work that takes me to the four corners of the earth, as well as two young boys that demand all of Dad's attention, I make sure that I have time to walk the few paths that cross the Berwyn hills with no one but my dogs, the wildlife, the scenery and the solitude to keep me company.

Y Berwyn

On This Mountain

# GARN FAWR
## Mererid Hopwood

You can scarcely call it a mountain. A moderately enthusiastic walker can reach its very summit in ten minutes without any sort of equipment, and even the straggler can do it in twenty.

You can see it for the first time as you travel towards the sea just north of Letterston, near the place where the A40 swerves to the left. There it is, sleeping, with its nose in the air, its hands crossed on its chest, and its toes tickling the clouds.

It bridges the divide between earth and sky, and defines the edge of the peninsula that is known today as Pencaer ('the headland of the fort'), but which was once known, so they say, as Pencawr ('Giant's Head'). And here lies that giant until this day. I believe that he was none other than Ysbaddaden himself, and we shall hear more of him before our journey ends.

But there, I have misled you already on two counts, not about Ysbaddaden, but about the term 'mountain'. First of all, it isn't really a mountain at all, but a *carn*, a cairn or heap of rocks, and secondly, it isn't even one *carn*, but four, if not six. The outline of this giant encompasses Garn Fawr, Garn Fechan, Garn Folch and Garn Gilfach, and his hillocky body hides Garn Bristgarn and Garn Gelli too. In fact, only one *carn* on the peninsula escapes his grasp, namely Garnwnda, and even that one was added to by another giant, none other than Samson. One stormy afternoon in a fierce rage he flung a huge stone from Garn Bristgarn all the way to Garnwnda, and that is why, even now, the striking cromlech on Garnwnda is known as Carreg Samson (Samson's Slab).

But of all these *cernydd*, ('outcrops' seems too matter-of-fact a name for the romance which is theirs), Garn Fawr is the tallest. It rises something over two hundred metres above the sea below – a dwarf in comparison to its cousin, Carn Ingli, a few miles away in the Preseli, but everything in this world is relative, and on a parcel of land as flat as Pencaer, this dwarf is a giant.

Wait until September and the early autumn before you climb Garn Fawr. It is more peaceful then, and to understand the place, you need peace. To get under its skin, you need tranquillity, and that can only be found after the summer – with its all-seeing, yet unseeing, visitors – is past.

To reach the summit from the east, you will follow a little lane – with its banks burdened with glistering blackberries at this time. Beneath your feet the ground seems hollow. Wait for a moment to strike the earth with the sole of your foot and you will hear an echo that tells you that here lies an old, old story. About halfway up, on your right, it is very easy for you to miss the little prehistoric well, especially if the fern is at its height. But it is there, hiding its crystal water under a lid of stone deep down in the earth. And when you find it, wait again, slake your thirst, and think of centuries of people who have met at this very spot. According to the experts, the first inhabitants came in the Stone Age – and that's a long, long time ago.

Back to the lane and keep climbing until you come to a dry-stone wall, where you will see, again on your right, a thick concrete needle. This triangulation point marks the highest place in Pencaer. To reach it, you must plough your own furrow through the heather and gorse. The odd patch of grass is like glass, so take care. Although the colour of the gorse is richer than that in the softest carpet, it would be more comfortable to land on the fiercest besom than in a bush!

Now, you can satisfy the urges of the daring adventurer in you by grasping the mighty stones between you and the summit to reach the apex like a Tensing.

And the prize? A world of wonder from horizon to horizon. Below you, St David's Head with its blister-like Clegyrn Boya

– named after the saint's only enemy; before you, Ireland, whence came that unfortunate man; Snowdonia and Bardsey on the other side and the Preseli range behind.

This is a strong *carn*, an ideal fortress. In the pattern of the stones you can see the skeleton of an Iron Age village, and in the incongruous concrete look-out, the skeletons of last century's two world wars. But in spite of the strategic vantage point you are afforded, there is one thing which remains a subject of wonder for the inhabitants of Pencaer. Although they can see the churches of many surrounding parishes – St. Nicholas, Grandston, Jordanston, Letterston, Hayscastle, Mathry – they can't see their own, Llanwnda.

Since it is September, and late in the afternoon, there are not many yachts at sea, especially if the water is streaked with white – and the Irish ferry went past at about three o'clock with Strumble lighthouse warning of the dangers of the rocks around St Michael's island.

The night is drawing closer, and the sun is putting on its golden stockings as it prepares to go to dance the day in some other place. It's what we call the 'tailor's hour', the time between times, when it's too dark to work by daylight but too light to set the candle. This is the time that the Garn is at its best as it casts its shadow long and lingering over the whole district. And this is the light that has attracted artists for

Garn Fawr

generations, in their midst John Piper, the artist of the windows of the new Coventry cathedral, and who owned Llys y Dryw ('the Wren's Court'), the smallest cottage that nestles in the shadow of the giant.

Below this cottage, to the southwest, is Pwll Deri, which is, as every good Welsh person knows, the home of the eagle, the bear and the bogey, or at least that's what the poet Dewi Emrys wrote. He knew it is a marvellous place to sit and ponder, and it was here that he saw the profligate angel pouring gorse like sovereigns over the cliff, and the good shepherd endangering his own life to save his lamb by chain and rope. This is where he thought of another Good Shepherd too.

Thanks to the conservation efforts of the National Park, the views from Garn Fawr are more or less the same as those in Dewi Emrys's time. By day at least. But if he returned today to ponder as the autumn night draws on, he would sense great changes as he looked from the summit at the plain below. In the empty houses of this headland there is no light; the cottages are blind. He would be flabbergasted that the rules of conservation are so concerned with the minutiae of the slates and the width of the gates, but care not a fig for the names of the places. For he would know that in the names lies the greatest richness of the place – Llan Fenws, Pwll Crochan, Penbwchdu, Trelimin, Tresisillt, Trenewy', Trehowel, Trehilyn, Trefaser . . .

Do you know who Aser was? None less than King Alfred's personal tutor and, according to Iolo Morganwg, his bardic name was Geraint Fardd Glas, one of the fathers of the grammar of strict-metre verse. And who was Hilyn who had his home in Trehilyn? None other than Heilyn, the son of Gwyn, from the story of Branwen, and it's only a stone's throw from Ynys Gwales, out at sea but within earshot of the bells of St. David's. (Ynys Gwales, known in English by the Viking Grassholm, but which literally means an island of shelter.)

Before we leave Pwll Deri, I want to remind you of Dôl Gâr and persuade you to pay it a visit to take a look at one of Wales's oldest dwellings. It is the sort of place that makes one wonder at the unwasteful snugness of the so-called primitives, and to ask oneself in all truth 'What is enough?' Bigger must be better according to today's gospel, but was it not Waldo, who lived in this very parish, who taught that to find 'a great hall between narrow walls' ('cael neuadd fawr rhwng cyfyng furiau') was the real secret?

Remember that these rocks were on the pilgrim's path to St. David's, and many a crossroad still bears an ancient 'milestone' showing a cross. These are known as Mesur y Dorth ('the loaf's measure'), presumably because they marked the spot where the pilgrims broke the bread for Holy Communion on their journey. Closer to St. David's, one whole village bears this name. There is no doubt that these ways have been trodden by thousands of feet over the ages.

This giant's kingdom may be small in area, but here there is a strange feeling of spaciousness too. After all, how many people in Wales can claim that their family once lived next door to the 'North Pole'? Honestly! That's exactly where Gwtws can be found, and Gwtws was my grandparents' first married home. In its turn, the cottage called North Pole looks down on the smallholding of Good Hope – a world away in half a mile! Surely the family who lived in Penrhyn, the next place down and nearest to the sea, showed faith as well as hope when they let their children out to play, tethered to prevent a catastrophic fall over the sheer cliff.

Garn Fawr

Follow the coastal path slowly from Penrhyn towards Strumble and you will reach a place called Capel Degen. You will not find a stone of this chapel, nor yet an altar, standing, but you will hear the memory of a slate slab that came to light under the heather, and an older memory of a monk who came ashore in his coracle after fleeing the destruction of Cantre'r Gwaelod, the drowned hundred of Cardigan Bay. The chapel is on the land of Tresinwen, and it is said that 'sin' is an old Welsh word for charity.

It's getting dark by now and I must hurry back to tell you of the giant himself, for although the starlight in Pencaer is pristine, I should not like to linger by myself on the Garn after nightfall.

Now, we have already talked of Ynys Gwales and Heilyn's home, and between these two places lies Porth Glais, a very important place in the (hi)story of the Mabinogi. It may not be possible for us now to prove the connection between this place and the story to the satisfaction of the cool-headed academic, but the heart has no doubts.

This, the heart, knows at once that it is true. It only has to hear that the old name for Garn Gilfach was Garn Culhwch, and that its neighbour is Garn Folch, which comes from the old Welsh word 'moloch' – a battle, and that the cromlech on that Garn is called Carreg Arthur, and again that there is a rock on Garn Bristgarn which is three feet wide, two feet deep and six feet tall, and that its name is 'Sêt y Cawr' (the Giant's Seat) – and it was here that Ysbaddaden would spend his days following Seithenyn's disastrous mistake when Cantre'r Gwaelod drowned.

The giant – Ysbaddaden Ben Cawr – had chosen his throne wisely, for although he knew that Garn Fawr was higher, he also knew that Garn Bristgarn gave a better view of north and west Wales and Cardigan Bay. And it was from this very seat that Ysbaddaden threw the stone, like a disc, which landed some half a mile to the south and gave its name to the farm called 'Goitan'.

In the same way, we can be certain that it was here that Culhwch finally came to grips with Ysbaddaden and shaved him with the scissors that once lay between the ears of the ferocious wild boar. And with the eyes of the heart, you can see him falling from his seat to disappear over the cliff into the sea. Yes, the seat is at an angle and has split, but it is still there, and the measurements are correct – so what do you expect when a giant in a rage falls from it?

With Ysbaddaden's disappearance, and Culhwch and Olwen's happy marriage, the evil spirit left Pencaer for ever, and that can be proved beyond doubt. Below Bristgarn is a lane – Feidr Pont Eglwys – and in the bank of that lane is a stone which shows the mark of the devil's hoof. Though moss and bramble may cover all the other stones in the bank, none has ever been seen over this stone, they would not dare to go near the hoofprint the evil one made as he leapt into the sea. This is truly a monument to the triumph of good over evil.

I suppose that that's why the old giant sleeps peacefully to this day, and it is a great comfort to realise that when the day arrives for him to wake again, at least he will be a kindly giant.

There is magic in Dyfed. And it is the magic of this mountain that draws me every time. When I was in primary school, I had to write a story telling what I should do if I was told that the world was going to end in three hours. At that

Garn Fawr

On This Mountain

time I was quite sure that I would go, with my family, as quickly as possible from Cardiff to Garn Fawr. And that's what I would do today too. I'm just as certain.

My advice to you, however, is don't wait for that warning before seeking the company of this rocky, kindly giant. Do it now.

Garn Fawr

On This Mountain

# MYNYDD Y GARREG

## Ray Gravell

What a mountain: Mynydd y Garreg is 'the mountain of stone' that gives my village its name and is found in one of Wales's most delightful valleys, the Gwendraeth.

It's a lovely location: on the coastal side of the cwm, we are exactly halfway between the county's two largest towns, with Llanelli nine miles to the east and Carmarthen, Wales's oldest town, nine miles to the west. A mile-and-a-half down the road is ancient Kidwelly, where the greater and lesser Gwendraeth rivers meander and merge in the marshland.

Our house is called Brynhyfryd ('Mount Pleasant'), a spot-on name given the spectacular views we enjoy from here. The Gower Peninsula is to the left, whilst to the right is Caldey Island, where the Irish established a monastery round about the fifth century. We're also lucky enough to overlook Kidwelly town itself and be made aware of the amazing history that surrounds us: here we see the conqueror's ruined castle, whilst St Mary's church tower too reminds us of its importance and dignity. Beyond these, Carmarthen Bay's ever-shifting blue carpet stretches to the horizon, to the land of mystery and magic. *Bois bach*, there's no beating this beauty!

Now, I was born in Kidwelly: Mam was from town and Dad from the mountain. Apparently we spent three months or so in the shadow of the old castle walls before Jac Gravell, my father, decided to return home, with Mam – Nina – and myself, naturally, in tow. And this, at six months of age, was my first introduction to that remarkable village built on firm, limestone foundations, Mynydd y Garreg.

We spent three years in a two-roomed whitewashed cottage called 'Bwlch y Mynydd' ('the mountain pass'), and my only memory of it is of our next-door neighbour, an amiable old man called Henry Hall. Apparently, Henry always looked out for the lively red-headed bundle, and would always refer to me as 'Redman'.

We subsequently moved from the outskirts to a brand-new council house; Mam was delighted with the sewerage system, the bath, the toilet – all the mod cons! 5 Bryn Hefin was a veritable mansion right in the middle of the village, with the Post Office nearby, along with two shops selling all kinds of goodies, and Aldwyn the Oil's garage open all hours night and day. I was a veteran four-year-old by now, my roots firmly planted and anchored in the close-knit community.

Mine was a very, very happy childhood and upbringing, without a care in the world, and with the certainty that Mam and Dad were always there looking after me and looking out for me. That, I believe, is the ideal childhood.

Now, right at the top of the village there was a cottage called 'Brynhyfryd' and Dad had set his heart on buying it. He was a collier, and worked at Pentre-mawr in Pontyberem, but his interests were trapping rabbits, gardening and supping a pint or two on Saturday night. A simple, honest and fulfilling life. Well, he was granted his wish and managed to buy the cottage, so off we went on the half-mile journey from the middle of the village to its top. Yes, Mynydd y Garreg was only a little village then: it's expanded considerably since the early 1950s, but, thankfully, a village it remains.

I was seven years old by now and part and parcel of village and community life. I'd also started to dabble with sport, rugby especially. As a former player, my father was delighted that I was following in his footsteps, and I was equally proud to be doing so. Dear Mam always fretted that 'Ray *bach*' would do himself a mischief chasing that oval ball. But she coped – as she had to – since rugby was a well-established way of life in this special cwm.

As well as rugby, my other great interest was hunting rabbits. I was never much of a gardener, but I was a dab hand at hunting, thanks to my father's influence and instruction. Those were unforgettable days: walking the mountain, nosing around the old quarries, helping out on farms, gathering the hay during the long, sweet days of summer, those captives of childhood memory – and all this in the company of my great hero, Dad.

I realise now that the backbone, the foundation of family life, was Mam, but Dad was the man for me, and the son did all he could to emulate him. Oh yes, he showed and taught me things that no college or university could have done; he shared secrets, he fostered a unique father-son relationship and gave me values, urging me to respect the community and its people. And, of course, he also passed on all that he knew of the area's history from the Norman invasion to the Industrial Revolution. He was also, as many colliers were, an occasional poet and loved music passionately.

Mam, on the other hand, was a townie, not quite so enthusiastic when it came to skinning rabbits, digging the garden and making *pele mond* (a mixture of small coal, clay and lime) to keep the fires alight for days on end. But, fair play to her, she knew her flowers and her ferrets! And whilst the garden overflowed with fruit and veg of every description,

Mynydd y Garreg

On This Mountain

Mam too had her own corner full of fine flowers, and a border brimming with a colourful concoction of fragrances that was enough to send the imagination on a magical journey to the depths of the sub-conscious. What a journey, what a sight, what an experience!

The village's Cae Post, a sloping, postage-stamp of a pitch, was our 'Theatre of Dreams', our cricket, rugby and football ground, our temporary Wimbledon even, where all the children of the village gathered and played. *Hwyl* and vibrancy, like the Cwm's coal seams, coursed through every single inch and acre of our village. Life was grand, the future was far away, and fraternity and friendship were treasured and appreciated – far more than gold and silver.

Unfortunately, however, fortunes were about to change. My father suffered an accident at Pentre-mawr pit, a serious accident that left not only its physical mark, but also a mental one. At the time, I was a pupil at the Boys' Grammar School in Carmarthen, playing rugby every Saturday: everything in my garden was rosy.

Then, one weekend, Dad took a walk along the mountain – and never returned. It was I who discovered his body, stiff and cold amongst the fern at the crest of the hill – a favourite haunt of ours when we hunted and ferreted for rabbits. He had committed suicide, the mining injury and subsequent depression proving too much for him.

I was fourteen years old when this happened. After his death, our lives were changed forever; but thanks to the help and support we received from friends and some members of the family, life had to go on, and on it went.

Mam was only forty years old, and the mountain was empty without Jac, so she decided she wanted to go back to Kidwelly. I pleaded with her not to take us away from Mynydd y Garreg because to me – selfishly as I was – without Dad, the cottage and the village, there was no future.

In her wisdom, Mam considered all things and decided ultimately that we should stay in Brynhyfryd.

I have nothing against Kidwelly – I was born there, after all – but it was in Mynydd y Garreg that I was raised. No one understands the fears and anxieties of a child better than a mother, and the debt I owe Nina Eileen Gravell is an eternal one. No wonder my father's words continue to echo in my ears: *'Cofia, dim ond un fam gei di, parcha hi'* – 'Remember,

you'll only ever have one mother, respect her.' Too true, Dad, too true.

Forty years have passed since his death. And during those forty years, well, so much has happened that it would take ages – and several volumes – to tell all the tales. I have travelled the globe playing rugby for Wales and the Lions, but the best journey, without a shadow of a doubt, remains the journey home.

Where is 'home'? Well, exactly where it's always been – Brynhyfryd, Mynydd y Garreg. When I was initiated into Gorsedd y Beirdd ('the Bardic Circle') at the Machynlleth National Eisteddfod in 1981, I took the bardic name 'Ray o'r Mynydd'. And, indeed, when my sweetheart, Mari, agreed to be my wife at Horeb chapel, Mynydd y Garreg in 1991 and insisted that Brynhyfryd should be our family home, I was over the moon. Mari and I now have two daughters, Manon and Gwenan, daughters of the mountain both, ensuring the future of all that they have inherited.

When Carmarthenshire County Council decided to name the road that leads to Brynhyfryd 'Heol Ray Gravell', Manon and Gwenan asked me a startling question: 'Dad, odi hynny'n golygu fyddi di'n byw am byth?' – *'Dad, does this mean that you'll live for ever?'* It was a question that sent me hurtling back to my childhood wandering the mountain by my father's side

Mynydd y Garreg

because, as an innocent child, I had always thought Dad would live for ever.

And I now understand the love that I felt towards my mother and father, and I see it and feel it in the love that my own children show to Mari and me.

So why does this mountain mean so much to me? I don't truly know the answer. But I do know this: I was born a son of the mountain and there is tranquillity here even in the eye of the fiercest storms. The mountain, so exposed and rocky, remains a fortress, providing refuge and support in times of worry and danger.

When friends or visitors call by, everyone, without exception, draws attention to the breathtaking views. And this reminds me, time and again that, yes, a father's dream has been fulfilled by the son: it was, after all, his vision that prompted me to try to make the ideal of living on this glorious mountain an everyday reality.

As I appreciate all that is around me and look back at what has been, I realise how privileged I have been to live where I have chosen to live. This may, of course, be because Mari, Manon and Gwenan share in it and feel passionately that this is their home too. And that's why it is more of a home to me now than it has ever been.

The late and dear Carwyn James, coach of the Lions and Llanelli, once told me: *'Raymond, rwyt ti'n ddyn dy filltir sgwâr'* – 'Raymond, you are a man of your square mile'. Carwyn was so right, and I am sure that I have carried that square mile and my Welshness with me on every journey and tour that I have undertaken. Carwyn also knew his people, and ultimately, it is people who make the place, and this mountain, Mynydd y Garreg, is the best place in the whole, wide world.

On This Mountain

# CRIB NANTLLE
## Dylan Iorwerth

The ravens accompany us. Past the old school and schoolhouse which, for most visitors are nothing more than that. The name, T.H. Parry-Williams on the slate plaque is no more than a pattern of letters and a hyphen. But the poet of the bare highlands heard the bird's guttural call too, almost like the rattle of death. He saw the breeze troubling Llyn y Gadair, just as it does now as we set off from the car park for Snowdon in the opposite direction. The ravens will always be there, raucous among the echoing rocks, rising like specks of ash up the wind's chimney and wheeling your head into a spin.

You come closer to yourself when you walk. The sucking sound of peat and sphagnum takes you back to childhood wanderings; the rushing river under the slate-slab bridge recreates adventurous sopping-wet days. This is Afon Gwyrfai, under your feet and then behind you as you use the clumps of reed as stepping stones over the boggy wetland to the foot of Y Garn.

Five miles downstream, and forty years back, we lived on her banks. Jumping the rocky islands, looking for a glimpse of trout in the black whirlpool of Pwll Tro and walking miles to see the wonder of the elvers crawling up the rocks at Nant y Betws on their instinct-driven odyssey to Llyn Cwellyn from the exotically resonant Saragasso Sea.

You can't see Llyn Cwellyn as you start your climb, only Llyn y Gadair, like a shard of broken mirror, on the grey and yellow heath. A little scrambling up the steep path brings a third lake into view – Llyn y Dywarchen, its name recalling the miraculous moving island that once used to float like a piece of turf on the water's surface.

This is the land of the Little People, hardier than fairies and more capricious. The open, wild expanse around Snowdon – Yr Wyddfa – is the Bermuda Triangle of Welsh folklore. Many young men were lost here and many mysterious beauties enticed them to never-land. Centuries ago, when only a few indistinct footpaths crossed this wilderness and only a few rough shelters offered the shepherds any solace in swirling mists, you can easily imagine being enchanted, caught between two worlds. Just as you are now.

Y Garn is the killer. It feels almost vertical, the path hacked and worn into ankle-twisting ditches and ravines. Even in winter now, the mountains get no respite. Today, as spring approaches, you can almost feel the water moving under the surface of the heather and coarse grass and, where the sun hasn't ventured, the rocks are treacherous. The first half-hour is the worst when all sounds are drowned by your gasping breath. At times, your tightening muscles tug you back, telling you to stop. Only your fear of giving up drives you on. Then, when your resolution begins to falter, the driving rhythm of your legs pushes you mindlessly upwards.

Steep climbs have their own reward. You see the landscape changing. The details slip away and the wider patterns take shape. You can see clearly where men have cut patches of bright green out of the heathland tweed, their edges fraying where the heather and reeds claw their way back. The rubble and the workings of quarries and copper mines seem like rips and gashes roughly stitched back by nature.

You need to set a target. Keep on to the next little ridge, then stop and stretch and look back where the whole of Snowdonia – Eryri – seems to rise like a pop-up book. As you climb, you see more. Eventually, almost all the peaks are in view; the nearest are sharp and well-defined, the farthest only liquid grey shadows in the distance. Moel Eilio over there on the left is the first of a string of round foothills shunting the eye towards brooding Clogwyn Du'r Arddu, where the steam

from the Snowdon train rises and flutters like a waving handkerchief. Moel Eilio was the backdrop to our childhood escapades, matching the curlew's angst-ridden soundtrack. Only the memory of that sound soars above the heather now.

Yr Wyddfa, of course, directly before you, is the centrepoint that holds all else together. From this angle, you wonder at its mass more than its height. The two Moelwyn peaks are to the right and Arennig way beyond. It is difficult to spot the Cnicht; from the west it may be Matterhorn-like, from here it is no more than an abrupt ending to a humdrum ridge. Perspective changes mountains.

From here, yr Aran – Snowdon's Aran – is close. The terrible ridge of Lliwedd creeps into view while, in a gap between cliff and peak, Elidir and the Carneddau draw the eye over the horizon where land merges into sky and you lose the difference between cloud and rock and ridge. Sometimes, as the day declines, these mountains look like wavy strips of grey and black paper layered in decoupage. There is nothing more theatrical than when a storm of thunder and lightning backlights them in silhouette.

You start walking again and one last surge takes you to the mountain wall and the stone-strewn moonscape leading to the first Nantlle peak. It is easy to believe those tales of giants carrying their sackloads of pebbles and dumping them in

Crib Nantlle

On This Mountain

places like this. What other explanation could yesterday's people have had for these unstable, uncomfortable screes? The ice caps and glaciers were gigantic in their own ways and only immense energy pushed shelves of rocks upwards and then froze and thawed them into these scattered pieces. Today's giants are helicopters, dropping their huge sacks of rocks to mend the ragged footpaths.

Suddenly, another new land appears underneath you, through abrubt gaps in the cliff edge. Another boundary between two worlds. There is the farm at Tal-y-mignedd and the pass at Drws-y-Coed. Down there, somewhere, are the remains of the tiny chapel that was crushed by a tumbling boulder and the derelict mineworkings that linger like a bitter memory. Above them, across the valley, is Craig y Bera, one side of Mynydd Mawr, the elephant-like mass that extends to our old stamping ground in Waunfawr. But, there, it's a different mountain.

And this is a different country. The land of Blodeuwedd, Gwydion and Lleu from the Mabinogion. Unlike the story, man may not have created life out of the flowers of the field, but he did so out of slate. Quarry rubble has covered one of the two lakes that gave Baladeulyn its name and the quarries of Nantlle may no longer be crawling with men, but you can still wonder at the energy that ripped those grey mounds of stone

from the grudging land and pushed shops and chapels and streets to the surface. The quarry landscape now looks like a deserted battlefield, all craters and scars – as if something terrible happened here because of man's defiance. Here, the raven called out many times and still does so when divers from the English cities lose their way, and their lives, in the water of Dorothea Quarry's great pit. Like those fabled shepherds disappearing into the arms of the Little People.

The cliff edges attract and repel, ledges tumbling one over the other into the green valley; they enchant and terrify. One moment, rain clouds are drawn over us like a grey shroud and, then, in the distance the sea is an expanse of light, with only the shadows of the clouds to darken it as they sail from the tip of Anglesey to the triple peaks of Yr Eifl and yet another world, in Llŷn.

It's time to turn back to the long ridge stretching out ahead of you; broad, then narrow, steep and then leisurely where the Nebo television mast stands like a finishing post. This next stretch, over Mynydd Drws-y-Coed to Trum y Ddysgl is the most exciting part of the walk, where arms and knees are active and the earth often disappears under you, within inches of your feet. But a view of Cwm Pennant is your prize and Ardudwy, amother fabled land, opens out ahead of you.

Crib Nantlle

*Cefn, ysgwydd, braich, ystlys* . . . back, shoulder, arm, side . . . the Welsh language has turned the mountains into living creatures and stories and histories are hidden in many of the names. Unsullied by anglicisation and the mindless renaming by climbers, they tell you of the people who used to live and work here, hardy shepherds or adventurous quarrymen and miners, carrying their experience of the mountains back with them in names and legends.

Underneath you now to your left is Bwlch-y-ddwy-elor, the pass of the two biers. No matter that experts now suggest another form of the name . . . it is better to believe the story about the funerals. When someone from Beddgelert, on one side of the pass, died in Cwm Pennant, on the other (or vice versa of course), it was at this spot, so they say, that the coffin would be handed over from the bier of one parish to the other. It's even less likely that, six hundred years after his revolt, Owain Glyn Dŵr is now hiding on Mynydd yr Ogof – the mountain of the cave – but living history isn't like that. As your eye skims from one barren peak to the other over towards Moel Hebog,

it's easy to imagine him turning for one last look at his land before settling to wait for his nation's call to action.

It's the noise that strikes you here. Lower down on the slopes, you hear very little, only the distant murmur of the main road and, perhaps, the howl of the Snowdon train. There are scarps and ridges to shut out the human hubbub.

But up here, where you can go no higher, where nature itself is silent, the constant tumult of our daily lives rises like a wave.

After the steep drop into the pass above Cwm y Ffynhonnau, where the springs of water were, the long path drags your eye up to Mynydd Tal-y-Mignedd. Drawing you on and breaking your heart. Sometimes, it's better not to see too much. But, ahead of you, a gap in a stone wall awaits, like an unanswered question. And the neat, stone monument built by unknown quarrymen is strange and out of place.

Most people go no further. There is a forbidding feel to Craig Cwm Silyn and the two dark lakes below. There's a sense of going beyond . . . beyond what, you hardly know.

Crib Nantlle

On This Mountain

Now there's only the sound of your boots on the loose stones and the rasping bleat of an occasional sheep echoing from the rocks, confounding your sense of direction. This is land where you should be alone, to sense the solitary and to know your place, to struggle down the scree and, if you lose sight of the path, to battle over mounds of heather and reed.

And then you reach Nasareth and Nebo, whose names create another strange world hundreds of miles and two thousand years away. From Nebo, you look back and upwards to the promised land.

Crib Nantlle

1. Mynydd Tynybraich
2. Mynydd y Gwrhyd
3. Cader Idris
4. The Blorenge
5. Cefn Du
6. Dinas Brân
7. Y Berwyn
8. Garn Fawr
9. Mynydd y Garreg
10. Crib Nantlle

# GUIDE TO THE IMAGES